LOVING HANDS
A 40-Day Devotional for Caregivers

LOVING HANDS
A 40-Day Devotional for Caregivers

Stephon C. Void

South Carolina United Methodist Advocate Press, Columbia, South Carolina
Copyright © 2024 by South Carolina United Methodist Advocate Press

All Scriptures taken from Common English Bible except otherwise noted.

Common English Bible. © Copyright 2011 Common English Bible.
All rights reserved.
Used by permission. (www.CommonEnglishBible.com).

Scripture quotations marked (NIV) are taken from The Holy Bible, New International Version, Copyright © 1973, 1978, 1984 by the International Bible Society. The Holy Bible, New International Version®, NIV® Copyright © 1973, 1978, 1984, 2011 by Biblica, Inc.® Used by permission. All rights reserved worldwide.

All rights reserved. No part of this book may be reproduced or transmitted in any form or by any means, electronic or mechanical, including photocopying, recording or by any information storage and retrieval system, without
permission in writing from the publisher.

First published in the United States of America in 2024 by the South Carolina United Methodist Advocate Press.

Library of Congress Cataloging-in-Publication Data
Loving Hands
p. cm.

ISBN 978-1-966237-02-0

This book is dedicated to all caretakers who tirelessly support their families.

Mom and Auntie Queen Ester, thank you for everything you do to keep our group together. We have looked out for one another for as long as I can remember. I love you both so much.

Aunts Joyce, Harriet, and Kristine, thank you for everything. Uncle Bobby, thank you for your support and wisdom.

Raunda, thank you for inspiring me to undertake this project.

Andre, you got this, big cousin. Thank you for standing in the gap time and time again.

Jessica and Shayla, you will be greatly blessed for what you are doing for your mom. Thank you for being there for us.

Rodrin, Shoperry, and Robert, thank you for being my bonus brothers.

To the Jim and Hannah crew, thank you so much for everything:

Cathy, Deron, Chris, Michael, Sharon, Ashley, Bernard, Elaine, Travis, and Rodney—growing up with you all has truly been a blessing. Thank you for standing in the gap.

To Aunt Charlese, Robin, Sonya, Jasmine, and Quenshawn, thank you for supporting Mom since Dad passed away. Y'all are the best.

Thomas "Hamp" Hamilton, thank you for being like a brother to my dad.

Monica, Sandy, and Kellye, Alma will not forget what you did for her.

To Pastor Sheri White and the New Covenant UMC family, you are my village, and I am who I am because of you all.

Sis. Betty Summers, thank you for all you have done for me and my mom.

Finally, Pastor Janice F. Watts, thank you for seeing the gift in me that I did not know I had.

Table of Contents

A Letter to Readers ix
Day 1: You Are Not Alone 1
Day 2: Be Patient with Them and Yourself 3
Day 3: Be Patient with God 5
Day 4: Find Rest 7
Day 5: Remember What Is Most Important 9
Day 6: It Is OK to Have Some Help 11
Day 7: Always Seek Heavenly Help 13
Day 8: God Is with You 15
Day 9: Stay the Course, God Will Provide 17
Day 10: God Hears Us 19
Day 11: God Has a Plan for You in This Season 21
Day 12: God Still Remembers Us 23
Day 13: Your Tears Will Turn into a Harvest 25
Day 14: Remain Slow to Anger 27
Day 15: All Things Work for the Good 29
Day 16: Choose Joy 31
Day 17: Don't Fall into Denial 33
Day 18: Letting Go of the Familiar and Embracing the New 35
Day 19: We Are in God's Plan 37
Day 20: Be Still 39
Day 21: Loving Hands 41
Day 22: Don't Get Tired of Doing Good 43
Day 23: Time Is Fleeting and Precious 45
Day 24: Thank You 47
Day 25: Seek Jesus in All Things 49
Day 26: Stay Connected to the True Vine 51
Day 27: May the Work of Our Hands Last 53
Day 28: Trust the Spirit in Tough Situations 55
Day 29: Be Godly with the Elderly 57
Day 30: Our Service Is a Symbol of Our Love and Faith 59
Day 31: A Plan for Saying Farewell 61
Day 32: Now What? 63
Day 33: This Is Not Our Home 65
Day 34: Your Heart Will Heal 67

Day 35: Get Plenty of Rest 69
Day 36: Restoration Is Coming 71
Day 37: Grief Will Not Be Your Identity 73
Day 38: Find a New Ministry to Do 75
Day 39: Remember the Professionals Who Helped You 77
Day 40: Find the Good in This Season 79
About the Author 81

A Letter to Readers

Dear Readers,

Thank you so much for picking up a copy of this devotional. This book is a continuation of my previous work, A Healing Journey: Poems of Faith, Healing, Recovery, and Grief. In that book, I shared my journey of being a caregiver for my dad, Carlisle, who was diagnosed with cancer in fall 2021 and passed away May 26, 2022. The book expressed what he and I went through as we both faced health struggles at the time.

My cousin Raunda gave me the idea to dedicate a book to those who care for a loved one when their health fails. Shortly after my father passed away, my mom's health also declined, and I found myself once again taking care of a parent. Caring for and then suddenly losing my dad took a toll on her physical and spiritual well-being. She took care of others and placed her own care on the back burner. I don't want others to do the same.

Being a caretaker for a spouse, child, grandparent, or parent can be a challenging task. Often, we feel alone or overwhelmed. For some, like my mom and myself, it can have a deep impact on our faith journey. This book is meant to be a help and a comfort, a reminder that God is with us through it all.

Why forty days? The number forty is associated with hardships and transitions to new beginnings. Noah was on the ark with his family for forty days and nights. The children of Israel traveled and wandered in the desert for forty years before they crossed over the Jordan River to the land of Canaan. Jesus was tempted and tested for forty days in the desert.

Being a health-care provider for a loved one is a journey. For some, it will lead to an earthly victory. For others, it's a journey that will lead to a long or short goodbye. Whatever the journey holds, this book is a constant reminder to lean totally on God for our strength.

I am not a theologian, nor have I attended seminary school. I'm just a humble layman who loves God and his fellow man. This book is a form of therapy for myself as I try to find balance in caring for my family and myself.

As we journey through these forty days together, I hope that we learn to fully rely on God and trust the promises he made.

I find that reading scripture and writing about my thoughts always helps me understand what God is trying to say to me. So, for this devotional series, I encourage you to read the focal passage for yourself and think about what God is trying to tell you each day.

I hope we all grow stronger in our faith as we embark on this forty-day journey together.

Yours in Christ.

—Stephon Void
November 2024

Day 1

You Are Not Alone

"I will do whatever you ask for in my name, so that the Father can be glorified in the Son. When you ask me for anything in my name, I will do it. If you love me, you will keep my commandments. I will ask the Father, and he will send another Companion, who will be with you forever."
—*John 14:13-16*

Read:
John 14.

Write:
How are feeling currently on your journey as a caretaker, and how does this scripture encourages you on this journey of care?

Some of you have just gotten the news that your loved one has an illness that has progressed, and they will need more hands-on care. Others of you may have been doing this for quite some time. No matter where you are on your journey with your loved one, it can be very emotional and stressful at times. There are doctor's appointments, new care regimens you must learn, and so many other things that might be involved. You must make sacrifices of time and resources to make sure the person you love so dearly has all the tools needed to have a quality of life they can enjoy. I get it because I've been there.

Sometimes we can feel like we are all alone and lost. It feels like we are in a constant state of alertness and wanting to do everything right. That anxiety we feel is normal. The disciples felt that way when Jesus foretold that he would be leaving soon. I can imagine they were concerned how they could carry on the ministry without Jesus being around. Then Jesus reassured them that as long as they remain faithful to the work they were called to do, he will always hear and answer their prayers. He also promised them the Holy Spirit would be there to guide and teach them forever and always.

My dear friends, the work that we do for our loved ones is a ministry that glorifies and honors God. He chose us to do this ministry because he knew we are loving and strong. There will be times we feel lonely, afraid, and like we don't have all the answers. There will be times we don't know how to cope or what to do. However, we will always have God the Father, God the Son, and God the Holy Spirit around to talk to. He will always listen, and he will answer in his own unique way. The answer may not always be what we want, but it will be exactly what we need to help us as ministers to the ones we love so much.

God will place the right people in our lives to help us get through this labor of love.

Let us pray:

God, we thank you for choosing us to be caregivers for those we love. At times we feel lonely and afraid because the path we are on is uncertain. We remain thankful and hopeful because we know we are not alone. We thank you for the gift of your Holy Spirit. May it continue to comfort and guide us when feel so uncertain. May we be forgiving of ourselves as we learn to understand this new chapter in our lives. In Jesus's name we pray, Amen.

Day 2

Be Patient with Them and Yourself

"Love is patient, love is kind, it isn't jealous, it doesn't brag, it isn't arrogant."—1 Corinthians 13:4

Read:
1 Corinthians 13

Write:
What do you think godly love is and how it can be applied to being a caregiver?

I get it. It is stressful at times dealing with people we care about. For those taking care of parents, this is a new normal for both of you. They are used to being independent. Now they can't do as much, and it scares them. Now they must relinquish their power to you, their child. That can cause friction.

The same goes for those caring for spouses. They don't want to see the love of their life giving up their normalcy and dreams to take care of them.

As a child growing up with my own health struggles, I felt like I was a burden at times. Then when I grew older and could take care of myself, my parents and other relatives had to get used to not doing all they used to do. As I gained more freedom, their worries shifted to what would happen if I did this or that. There are so many scenarios that can cause tension or anxiety.

Then there is the self-defamation and doubt that we as caregivers go through. We question every little detail about daily routines. We scrutinize every medical report. If we must assist with mobility, we are tense because we worry about our loved one falling or getting hurt. We feel like we aren't doing enough and that we are failing our family if we miss any little detail. We can be our own worst critics, and that's not good.

That's when we should remember why and for whom we are doing this. We are doing this task because we love them. We are doing it because they would do the same for us. We are doing it because we cherish them as precious gifts God gave us. That's why we must be patient with them and ourselves.

When the arguments or setbacks come, just remember you love them and so does God. If we can just slow down, take a breath, and think about things clearly, we can do our ministry of love more effectively.

Let us pray:

Heavenly Father, teach us to have patience in the way you have had patience with us. Guide our hearts and minds as we strive to be the best caretaker for our loved ones. We may not always be right, and other times, things may be smooth sailing. Help us to understand it is OK. In your name we pray, Amen.

Day 3

Be Patient with God

"But those who hope in the Lord will renew their strength; they will fly up on wings like eagles; they will run and not be tired; they will walk and not be weary."—Isaiah 40:31

Read:
Isaiah 40

Write:
Journal about how the prophet's reassurances inspire you.

Isaiah 40:31 is one of my favorite scriptures. It is a constant reminder that no matter what, if you are patient and hopeful, God will restore what you have lost in a challenging time.

Being a caretaker can be costly financially, emotionally, physically, and spiritually. There may be times when you are in a constant state of prayer and frustration. You may even question if you are strong enough to do it all. At times you may even question why God placed this calling on you and your family.

It can be tough managing a home, kids, marriage/singlehood, work, church, and taking care of someone you love dearly. No matter how hard it gets, we must remember God still hears us and he still cares. Our current circumstances should not hinder us from knowing that better days are coming. We can't allow temporary setbacks to blind our spiritual eyes to that fact that God is working behind the scenes to make all things better. We must not let worry, fear, and anxiety have more power than our faith in God.

During this stage of our lives, we should remain hopeful. It will not always be a hard road. Our season of lack will be replaced with more than enough. Our dark cloudy days will be replaced with sunshine.

When we are tired and worn out, God will give us the strength to press forward. Our tears of frustration and sadness will be replaced with tears of joy. We just must wait on God's timing and remain faithful.

Let us pray:

Father God, thank you for being a loving, kind, and restorative God. Please continue to give us your blessed assurance that everything will be OK. We praise you for what you have done and will continue to do during our faith journey with our family members. May you continue to be a beacon of hope during our dark times. Help us to remain patient and hopeful in this ministry of love. In your name, Amen.

Day 4

Find Rest

"He lets me rest in grassy meadows; he leads me to restful waters."
—Psalm 23:2

Read:
Psalm 23

Write:
Think of ways you should rest and plan to do it.

Rest is such a simple word; however, it is so hard to do. In America, we have been programmed to always work hard. We are told if we work hard enough then we can get to where we want to be. We push ourselves to the limit day in and day out. We try our best just to get ahead so we can be comfortable. This attitude trickles down to our home life, our children's school life, and now this new phase of life of being a caretaker. It is not healthy, and it is not safe.

We should not feel guilty about resting. God wants us to rest. In Genesis, God rested on the seventh day and made it holy. Jesus was mentioned resting several times in the Gospels. He even managed to sleep in the middle of a storm. So if God the Father and God the Son find time to rest, then why can't we? Why do we feel so guilty for taking a nap or planning a vacation? Why do we feel anxious because we put off our chores for one afternoon to catch a movie or binge watch a show?

Yes, our work is important. Yes, we love our family. But we are no good to them in a hospital bed of our own. Repeatedly I have witnessed the caregiver get sicker than the person they are caring for or even die before them.

We should not only rest our bodies, but we should rest our minds and souls as well. That means we must shut off the phones and tablets. It means we should do what we are doing now—reading a book to develop a closer connection with God. It means taking a walk without earbuds or headphones.

When we renew our minds and grow closer with God, we become rejuvenated. When our minds, bodies, and souls are rested, we can have the energy needed to minister to our loved ones.

Our life with family shouldn't be confined to checking off a to-do list. It should be about making more meaningful memories while we still can do so. So let us make a vow of getting away from it all (at times alone and others with family). Say it with me, friends, "It's OK to take a break."

Now go and plan something awesome to do for you, and then find something you can do with your family.

Let us pray:

Father, help us to find physical and spiritual rest in you. Help us to not feel guilty for doing so. We thank you for being the good shepherd who leads us to the quiet streams and grassy fields. May your word inspire us all to have a healthy life balance. In your name we pray, Amen.

Day 5

Remember What Is Most Important

"The Lord answered, 'Martha, Martha, you are worried and distracted by many things. One thing is necessary. Mary has chosen the better part. It won't be taken away from her.'"—Luke 10:41-42

Read:
Luke 10:38-42

Write:
Think about yourself. Are you more like Mary or Martha? Or are you a combination of both?

This is Part 2 of yesterday's devotional. Mary and Martha are two impactful women in the ministry of Jesus. When we are first introduced to them in Luke, we see their personality. Martha is the hard working, by-the-book sister. Mary, on the other hand, is the more passionate sister. From their personalities, I can guess Martha is the oldest of the two. Both show their love for their dear friend Jesus, but one remembers what is most important. Mary realizes the importance of spending time with the people we care about.

Like Martha, we can become distracted by the work we have to do as a caretaker. We forget at times to be present in the moment with our loved ones like Mary. We see the to-do list of chores and tasks, and we focus more on that instead of seeing all our loved one needs sometimes is our presence and time.

There is no doubt the work must be done so we don't hinder care or let our houses get messy. However, everything does not need to be a regimen. We should stop and share moments with the people we love.

We need to carve out time to just sit and enjoy our moments with our loved ones. We should pull out photo albums and remember the good old days. If we are taking care of kids, we should do fun activities that will take their minds off being different. Taking walks or including our loved ones in their care (if they are able) are meaningful ways we can live in the moment with our family members.

The time we have could be days, months, or years, but it is still short. Let's continue to find more ways to focus on the people we love and not all the work that goes along with it.

Finding the right balance will be beneficial to us all on this journey.

Let us pray:

Lord, help us to be more present in our time with you and with our loved ones that you have given us. Help us to cherish each moment and remember what matters most in our labor of love. In your name we pray, Amen.

Day 6

It Is OK to Have Some Help

"Moses's father-in-law said to him, 'What you are doing isn't good. You will end up totally wearing yourself out, both you and these people who are with you. The work is too difficult for you. You can't do it alone.'"
—*Exodus 18:17-18*

Read:
Exodus 18:13-24

Write:
Reflect on whether you have a support system. If not, why?

Yes, it's the third day in a row we are focusing on work. I don't care how qualified or trained we are. We cannot and must not think we are alone in this.

Moses had the luxury of his father-in-law's advice about appointing judges to handle smaller cases. He saw the toll the work was taking on Moses. By delegating the work, Moses could rest and be more of the leader he was called to be.

As caretakers, it is important to have a support system in place. Like I said before, it can be easy to fall into an intense routine and forget to take care of ourselves. We also neglect other relationships and duties, and that can cause a strain on ourselves.

We must remember to ask for help. We can ask our spouses, significant others, other siblings, and the like to help sometimes. In cases where we can no longer do it alone, we may have to bring in outside help. When we can't find internal help, then it may be prudent to have trained outside help. That does not mean we don't love our family any less. It just means we are loving enough to see we can't do it all by ourselves.

I'm forever grateful to my aunts, cousins, and church family for being my helpers. I have one aunt who takes my mom to her appointments and helps my mom when I need to work. Another has provided meals for us when we couldn't cook. My cousins have come over to help my mom with her hair because I can barely brush mine. Others have helped me with repairs or donated funds because they live far away. Each helping hand has taken a lot of stress off me, and I praise God for them all.

Providing care to our loved ones is a ministry, but it is not our identity. Some of us are married or dating and have children. Then we also have friends and coworkers who are important to us as well. We also have a personal responsibility to have a relationship with God and his son Jesus.

To maintain all those roles in a healthy way, we should be willing to accept help. Even Jesus had help, and he was the Son of Man.

We cannot lose ourselves in this ministry; that can fuel unhealthy emotions and soon cause tension in our homes. Asking for help is not taking the easy way out. It is a form of self-care and self-love.

Let us pray:

Heavenly Father, we thank you for giving us the wisdom to seek help when we need it. Help us to build lasting relationships with all we care about. Help us not to lose ourselves and to remember who we are and to whom we belong. In your name we pray, Amen.

Day 7

Always Seek Heavenly Help

"I raise my eyes toward the mountains. Where will my help come from? My help comes from the Lord, the maker of heaven and earth."
—Psalm 121:1-2

Read:
Psalm 121

Write:
How does this scripture makes you feel about God being a present and consistent helper?

When life gets us down, we should look up. We should seek God's heavenly counsel.

So many times, we feel like we can handle it on our own. We search, and we work extra hard. In the end, we finally realize what we should have done was talk to God first. We wasted so much time and effort trying to fix a God-sized dilemma without God.

We are always told to seek the manufacturer of a product to service it. If our car needs maintenance, we seek a mechanic. When our house has a leak, we call a plumber. When our electronics are damaged, we call the Geek Squad.

God created us. We should seek him to help us understand what is going on with our problems. The unique thing is we don't have to travel to seek him out. All we need to do is pray wherever we are.

There may be times when the answer may not come right away. There will also be times when the answer we seek will not be what we want. There will also be times when the person we least expect will be sent by him to help us solve the issue.

Whatever, wherever, or however God's answer manifests itself, the answer will be just what we need in that moment.

Let us pray:
God, thank you for always being a constant help in our time of need. Help us to remember to consult you first when things become overwhelming. Help us to be willing to accept your answer whatever it may be. In your name we pray, Amen.

Day 8

God Is with You

"But the Lord is the one who is marching before you! He is the one who will be with you! He won't let you down. He won't abandon you. So don't be afraid or scared!"—Deuteronomy 31:8

Read:
Deuteronomy 31:8

Write:
How does this make you feel?

A common feeling as a caregiver is loneliness. It often feels like we are on an island of our own making. We are part of a club no one asked to be in.

Our loved one has a condition that has no cure, or they are suffering from what the cure is, and we must do our best to give them the best quality of life. The once-vibrant person is now a shadow of who they used to be, or they never will have the chance to live the life you had hoped for them.

It is a lot.

We often ask ourselves, "Where is God in all of this?" The answer is that God has always been there. Life is not a perfect story. It has hills and valleys. It has happy days and sad days. It has setbacks and seasons of disappointments. God has been with us through it all. He already knew what we had to face before we got to the situation and knows how it's going to end. We simply must trust him in all of it.

The quiet moments, when we can't feel him, are the hardest. We question everything, and we often question him. In those moments we must remember that God is still there. He's still guiding us. Most importantly, he still loves us.

Time and life are fleeting, but God's love for us remains steadfast. We need to hold on tight to that love in these uncertain times.

Let us pray:
God, thank you for being there before, during, and after this time of uncertainty. Continue to reassure us that everything will be OK. Comfort us when we feel alone. Keep us on the right path as we try to be there for our loved ones. In your name, Amen.

Day 9

Stay the Course, God Will Provide

"The widow went and did what Elijah said. So the widow, Elijah, and the widow's household ate for many days. The jar of flour didn't decrease nor did the bottle of oil run out, just as the Lord spoke through Elijah."
—*1 Kings 17:15-16*

Read:
1 Kings 17:7-16

Write:
Reflect on the widow's story and how her faith in God and Elijah sustained her through a tough time.

The widow in 1 Kings 17 was praying to God for weeks prior to meeting Elijah. Every day she hoped her Jehovah Jireh would come through for her. Day after day, she knew her grain and oil jar would continue to diminish. She didn't have a male relative on which she could rely. It was just her, her young son, and her faith.

The very moment she nearly gave up on God, God stepped in a provided miracle through the prophet Elijah.

At first, she was skeptical and afraid, but she still trusted in God. She trusted God even though it did not make sense, and she was rewarded for her faithfulness.

Being a caretaker means you must stretch your resources. Unexpected expenses will come, and that's OK. Why is it OK? It is OK because God will provide somehow and some way. We have a ministry to give, and God will not leave nor forsake us. When we get to the point of losing hope, he will step in to make a way out of no way.

When my dad was admitted for surgery to remove the tumor from his tongue, he faced four weeks of recovery in a hospital. The hospital was two and a half hours away from home. We stayed every other week in a hotel. We never wanted for anything because God sent angels in disguise of family and friends. Our oil and grain never ran out.

When my dad succumbed to his fight against cancer and post-traumatic stress disorder, and my mom was in the hospital a few days later, my oil and grain never ran out. When my mom got diagnosed with Stage Four kidney disease and had to go on peritoneal dialysis, our oil and grain did not run out.

Repeatedly, I've teetered on the brink of losing all hope. God has always stepped in with exactly what I needed. When I thought our jars would be bare, here comes Jehovah Jireh once again to give us just enough.

So when I tell you "God will provide," I am speaking from experience. My friends, we must stay the course and trust that God will provide.

Let us pray:

God our provider, thank you for always stepping in when our resources are low. Thank you for always showing up overshadowing our fears and anxiety. Thank you for being that constant reminder that you are with us. In your name I pray, Amen.

Day 10

God Hears Us

"But me! I will keep watch for the Lord; I will wait for the God of my salvation; my God will hear me."—Micah 7:7

Read:
Micah 7:1-7

Write:
How can you relate to the prophet in this passage?

Micah is not often quoted in many sermons or devotionals unless it's about tithing. I've read this book, but nothing pierced my heart until now. We get new revelations every time we read God's word. This is what God has revealed to me for you and me today: He hears us.

In this world we are bombarded with politics, racial tensions, war, and a fluctuating economy. We never know if this next trip at a festival, shopping center, concert, or school event will be our last because of gun violence. Our sanctuaries are no longer safe havens because of worldly violence. The memories of Mother Emanuel and the Charleston Nine are still fresh in our minds.

No matter what goes on as we carry out our labor of love, we can always find peace in knowing God hears us.

It's so easy to become distracted by the chaos of the world around us. Micah reminds us that if we block out the negativity and seek out God, he will hear our cries for help. The world can be crumbling around us, but God's ears are still open to our prayers. He can see our tears, and he acknowledges our pain. Our focus should remain on the one who can quiet the storms and calm the waters.

As we care for our loved ones, there will be times filled with calamity and uncertainty. The comfort in knowing God still hears us and loves us can give us the motivation we need to face anything.

The difficulties of this world will come and go, but the love of God will outlast them all.

Let us pray:

God, thank you for being a kind ear that listens during all the distractions of the world. Help us to remain calm and still during it all. In your name we pray, Amen.

Day 11

God Has a Plan for You in This Season

"My plans aren't your plans, nor are your ways my ways, says the Lord. Just as the heavens are higher than the earth, so are my ways higher than your ways, and my plans than your plans."
—Isaiah 55:8-9

Read:
Isaiah 55

Write:
What are the scriptures saying to you in this season of caring for your loved one?

I can imagine what we are doing now was certainly not the plan for our lives when we were kids and teens. We didn't plan on our parents and grandparents getting old. We did not plan to have a child with special needs. We did not plan for our spouse to come down with cancer or a disease we cannot spell. We are in the prime of our lives, the age where we have worked as much as we should work, and it is supposed to be our time. Being someone's caregiver was not the hand we wanted dealt to us.

Well, God had another plan for you and me. We had this hand of cards dealt to us, and we still must play the game. If you are a spades player like I am, you know that sometimes a bad hand can turn into the game-winning hand. We can make the best out of a tricky situation by taking each day as it comes and trusting in the plan that God has for us.

Believe it or not, we were meant to be in this season doing what we are doing right now. God knew what he was doing. He chose us for this purpose. He knew we could be trusted to do what is right and pleasing for him. Everything we are doing is working for the glory of God. We worship and honor him by giving the people we love the best care.

I cherished every moment with my dad in his final year, and we didn't always agree on how to get things done. I gave him my best, and now I'm doing my best with my mom. Again, we never agree on everything, and things don't always go as planned, but I know I'm honoring both God and her by doing my best.

I don't know what God has in store for my family or your family in the future, but it is my prayer that we stick to God's plan. I pray that we trust him enough to fulfill it.

We know the work is not easy, but it is rewarding to know that in this season of life, we are fulfilling God's purpose for our lives.

Let us pray:

God, we thank you for choosing us to be a part of your plan. Help us to cherish each step of the process as it comes. We give thanks for the love you pour into us so we can share it with the people we care for. In your name we pray, Amen.

Day 12

God Still Remembers Us

"God remembers his covenant forever, the word he commanded to a thousand generations, which he made with Abraham, the solemn pledge he swore to Isaac."—Psalm 105:8-9

Read:
Psalm 105

Write:
How do you feel knowing God still remembers us and his promises to us?

Dementia is a cruel disease. All it does is take, take, and take some more. Those of you who are going through this now, I empathize with you. Every day you see that once-bright soul slowly go dim. The biggest fear most have is, "Will my loved one remember me tomorrow?" Then there is a glimmer of hope when they remember something, and just like that they go back to that same blank stare.

It's enough to make anyone want to break down and cry.

That is when we look to scripture to find reassurance and peace. Psalm 105 gives us that glimmer of hope. It reveals to us that, even through thousands of generations, God will not forget the promises he made to us. The promises of Abraham are now living in each of us—promises of unthinkable favor and unwavering grace. Those promises were fulfilled in the life, death, and resurrection of Jesus Christ.

Because the grave is empty, we are free of our old selves, and we are adopted into God's heavenly family. Because God has kept his promises, we can have the assurance of knowing our loved ones will be free of this horrible disease soon and will be welcomed home and restored to a full life. Because Christ rose, we can remain hopeful that we will see our restored family member again in the new Jerusalem.

So my dear friends, your loved one's mind may be fading, and their memories may fade. But God's promises are there to remind you that better days are coming for you and for them. Don't get weary of doing your best for them. They still love you; they just can't express it the same way anymore.

God sees your faithfulness, and he will be there to comfort you every step of a way.

Let us pray:

Dear God, thank you for remembering us and for keeping every promise. Help us to remember that when times get tough on this journey. Thank you for sending your son to be a living representation of fulfilling that promise. In your name, Amen.

Day 13

Your Tears Will Turn into a Harvest

*"Let those who plant with tears reap the harvest with joyful shouts.
Let those who go out, crying and carrying their seed,
come home with joyful shouts, carrying bales of grain!"*
—Psalm 126:5-6

Read:
Psalm 126

Write:
How do you feel knowing God sees our tears and turns them into blessings of harvest?

Tears come with the territory of being a caregiver. It hard to not to show emotion especially in this calling on our lives. We remember who our loved ones used to be. We remember what it was like to see them smile and to be carefree. Now they are prisoners to their current condition.

Some have a willing mind, but their bodies are not the same. Others are also losing their mental faculties. Parents of children are just trying to understand how their children experience this world and how they can help them live in it.

Whatever the case, maybe we mourn with and for our loved ones. We, like the Israelites who were in exile, long for better days and for restoration. This season of our lives is uncertain and can be incredibly stressful. We get full, and we cry physically and spiritually. Sometimes we don't even know why the tears fall.

Today I want you to know that God sees, and he acknowledges our tears. This season, like all seasons, will soon end. God is going to use those tears to water the soil of our future harvest in our next season. Our next season will be a season of abundance and growth because we were faithful in helping our loved ones have a better quality of life.

This ministry that seems cumbersome will one day be replaced with a season of unspeakable joy and peace.

Let us pray:

Abba Father and the Lord of the harvest of plenty, we are thankful you are using our tears of anxiety, sadness, and fear to water the seeds of the next season. May our next season be full of the harvest of the many promises left unfilled in our lives. May we enjoy the fruits of our labor. Grant us the strength to continue the work we have blessed to do. In your name we pray, Amen.

Day 14

Remain Slow to Anger

"Know this, my dear brothers and sisters: everyone should be quick to listen, slow to speak, and slow to grow angry. This is because an angry person doesn't produce God's righteousness."—James 1:19-20

Read:
James 1:19-20

Write:
How can you find ways to be less reactive to situations?

Our family members always know what buttons to push, don't they? It could be intentional or it could be unintentional. Either way, they can really get our blood boiling.

Whether things escalate to all-out war depends on how we react to the situation. The question we should ask ourselves is "Is it worth it?"

Words and actions can hurt. It hurts the most when those words come from people we love and care for deeply. I can recall a few times my parents and I had heated conversations. I always felt like I had to defend myself because I knew I was doing my best and it hurt me when they thought otherwise. Instead of yielding, I gave as much as they did. However, that wasn't healthy nor godly. It hurt me more than it hurt them.

Instead of listening in order to react, we must listen in order to figure out why our loved one felt that way. They are lashing out for reasons that might not even be about us or what we did or did not do. Maybe they are in pain or in a season of self-guilt. They don't know how to channel their anger, and unfortunately, we catch the brunt of it.

What we can also do is be big enough to apologize or walk away for a while. Once the adrenaline is out of our system, we can pray and ask God to help us understand the situation form our loved one's perspective. We are all human and we get angry, but we have the gift of the Holy Spirt that can help us channel our anger into a positive direction.

We must remember that we are a team and we have the same goal.

Let us pray:
God, please help us to listen with our ears and meditate what was said before reacting to a situation. Help us to not take everything personally and remember that we are on the same team and focused on the same goals. Help us to see each other's point of view. Help us to remember who we are and to whom we belong. In your name, Amen.

Day 15

All Things Work for the Good

"In the same way, the Spirit comes to help our weakness. We don't know what we should pray, but the Spirit himself pleads our case with unexpressed groans. The one who searches hearts knows how the Spirit thinks, because he pleads for the saints, consistent with God's will. We know that God works all things together for good for the ones who love God, for those who are called according to his purpose. We know this because God knew them in advance, and he decided in advance that they would be conformed to the image of his Son."
—Romans 8:26-29

Read:
Romans 8:26-29

Write:
How do you find hope even in this season of your life?

Despite how we may feel today, there is some goodness in this day. It might be a difficult day overall. Something or everything we have tried to do today might have not has gone as planned. Despite all of that, there is still good in this day. There is something to shout about.

We still have hope in Jesus Christ. He gave us another day. He gave us this moment to cherish our loved ones. He died and rose again to claim victory over every moment that causes us grief. Every lash, every nail, and every drop of blood shed was for all of us. We have goodness because Jesus our savior is good. So when we have those moments we don't understand, we must seek the goodness in it.

God has a divine plan for us all. Sometimes that plan includes bumps in the road. That road might be riddled with bad test results, disappointments, and sadness. However, we have survived every sad thing we have experienced so far. Everything we have endured and witnessed in our lives has prepared us for this season of love and service. The work we are doing now will be a story of triumph for a nonbeliever or someone who is struggling with the same situations. There is good in our struggle.

So let's focus on finding those glimmers of hope. God is going to use them to deliver others. Brother Paul was right. All things will work for the good.

Let us pray:

Father, we thank you for every aspect of our lives, the good and the bad. May our bad days turn into a story of faith. May our setbacks prepare us for a comeback. May our mourning turn into dancing. In your name we pray, Amen.

Day 16

Choose Joy

"Be glad in the Lord always! Again, I say, be glad! Let your gentleness show in your treatment of all people. The Lord is near. Don't be anxious about anything; rather, bring up all your requests to God in your prayers and petitions, along with giving thanks. Then the peace of God that exceeds all understanding will keep your hearts and minds safe in Christ Jesus."
— *Philippians 4:4-7*

Read:
Philippians 4:4-7

Write:
How will you choose joy today?

I feel like anyone who knows about finding joy is Paul. He laid his life and body on the line repeatedly. From snake bites to shipwrecks and imprisonments, Paul endured so much to reach the world and to spread the gospel of Jesus. What he did was not easy, yet he rejoiced in the power of God.

As caretakers, we face tough days. Some days we just want to just sit alone and cry. The world can feel like it's crumbling around us from the pressure of being the one who makes the decisions for our loved one's care. That's why Paul encourages us to seek God in prayer and to seek his peace in the chaos of our lives. He knows only God can fix some of the problems we face daily.

When the doctor's report is not good, we will choose joy. When we or our family member is having a rough day, we will choose joy. On the days we can't find the answers, we will pray, seek God's peace, and still rejoice. Why? We will do so because God is near and present. He always responds to our prayers, and the joy of the Lord is our refuge.

When we have that God-given joy, it overflows, and it spreads to the people we see and love every day. It encourages us to serve our purpose.

Let us pray:

Father, we thank you for being the source of our joy. We thank you for being the peace that surpasses all understanding. Help us to seek and spread joy in any way that we can. In your name, Amen.

Day 17

Don't Fall into Denial

*"Peter responded, 'Man, I don't know what you are talking about!'
At that very moment, while he was still speaking, a rooster crowed.
The Lord turned and looked straight at Peter, and Peter remembered the
Lord's words: 'Before a rooster crows today, you will deny me three times.'
And Peter went out and cried uncontrollably."*
—Luke 22:60-62

Read:
Luke 22:54-62

Write:
How do you feel about what's currently going on with your faith walk as a caretaker? Are you embracing it or in a state of denial?

Peter was in a tough situation. He placed his foot in his mouth and said he would never betray Jesus, but Jesus told Peter he would deny Jesus three times before the rooster crowed. Then Jesus was arrested, and sure enough—Peter denied knowing Jesus three times before the rooster crowed.

In tough situations, we lean toward sheltering our minds like Peter was trying to protect his life. It's not healthy nor beneficial for us to do so.

When I heard the words from my dad's doctor stating he had late-stage tongue cancer, I knew my life would forever change. I didn't question God at the time. I prayed God would equip me and my family to do whatever it took to restore him to a better quality of life.

When I got the news of him being in septic shock because of an infection and that he would not make it, I prayed again for God to strengthen us for what whatever would come. I was blessed to accept the reality that was before me.

Unfortunately, many fellow caregivers often fall into a period of denial. It is a coping mechanism and a way to delay the reality in front of them. They, like Peter, use it as protection.

My friends, I'm asking that we have a spirit of asking God for help with dealing with current circumstances and not hide ourselves in a cocoon. The current circumstances we face will not just simply go away; God must provide the healing. We must be strong enough to accept how that healing may be. The sooner we embrace it, the sooner we as caregivers can be available to be a source of strength for our loved ones.

My dad received healing by going home with God. It was a hard pill to swallow. I loved him, and he was my hero and champion. However, by allowing God to be God and embracing the reality of it, I was at peace. I saw the pain my father endured, and I saw the toll the radiation took. I knew this was the healing he needed.

I'm aware all of us are not in that stage of trust on our faith journey. Some of us are like Peter, hoping for a better or different outcome. It took Peter a while to accept his new reality. But when he did, he became a champion and leader in the life of the church.

God is calling us to be a champion for the ones he trusted us to care for. Let us embrace what we must deal with and trust in God's will. For some of us, that means earthly healing, and unfortunately for others, it means helping them transition to a better place free from their pain.

Let us pray:

God, we thank you for being all we need in our lives. Help us to embrace reality and still cling to our faith. Help us not to deny your will and be strong enough to know you always know what is best. Help us to turn to you and not fall into a trap of fear and denial. In your name we pray, Amen.

Day 18

Letting Go of the Familiar and Embracing the New

"When they finished eating, Jesus asked Simon Peter, 'Simon son of John, do you love me more than these?' Simon replied, 'Yes, Lord, you know I love you.' Jesus said to him, 'Feed my lambs.' Jesus asked a second time, 'Simon son of John, do you love me?' Simon replied, 'Yes, Lord, you know I love you.' Jesus said to him, 'Take care of my sheep.' He asked a third time, 'Simon son of John, do you love me?' Peter was sad that Jesus asked him a third time, 'Do you love me?' He replied, 'Lord, you know everything; you know I love you.' Jesus said to him, 'Feed my sheep.'"—John 21:15-17

Read:
John 21:3-19

Write:
How are you accepting your new or current season as a caregiver? How does it compare to Peter accepting his new leadership role in ministry?

Today we are continuing to look at how Peter is handling overwhelming news. Previously he denied Christ three times. In this situation, Peter was overwhelmed by the resurrection of Jesus and his soon departure from earth. He and the disciples were in hiding from the Jewish leadership. His future seemed uncertain. So to cope, he went back to what was familiar to him. He went fishing with the other disciples.

His trip wasn't fruitful. Nothing happened until Jesus showed up. The catch was plentiful, and Jesus even had breakfast prepared for them.

Jesus had a conversation with Peter and three times asked Peter about his love for him. Each time Peter replied, "Yes, I love you." In response, Jesus replied, "Feed my sheep."

With this, Peter received his new assignment and charge. He was to feed the lost sheep of the world. He was to do so by showing his love for Christ to others by sharing the good news of redemption and salvation. The fireside pep talks and huge bounty of fish were a sign of good faith that Jesus trusted Peter to do the right thing when the time came.

As caregivers, we often want to run back and cling to the old way of life. The reality is we now have a new assignment and a new calling on our lives. We are to share in God's love and grace by giving the best care for our loved ones. That means that we may have to adjust our schedules or make sacrifices we never thought we had to do.

The road ahead is uncertain and at times it can be overwhelming. We can and will do our best because God is with us. If Peter never embraced his calling, where would the church be now? If we don't accept and embrace this period of service and love, what will we do to our soul and heart?

By letting go of what's familiar and embracing this call on our lives, we will be rewarded with many blessings. Some we may see outwardly, and others we may never know about. We may feel unqualified or that we are not strong enough, but the Holy Spirit who lives in us will give us the strength, courage, and wisdom we need to be there for our family.

Let us pray:

God of bountiful blessings and hope, we thank you for the blessing of this day. Guide us as we try to navigate this journey of love and care. Continue to strengthen and encourage us as we embrace this ministry that we are called to do. Amen.

Day 19

We Are in God's Plans

*"I know the plans I have in mind for you, declares the Lord;
they are plans for peace, not disaster, to give you a future filled with hope.
When you call me and come and pray to me, I will listen to you.
When you search for me, yes, search for me with all your heart,
you will find me."—Jeremiah 29:11-13*

Read:
Jeremiah 29:11-13

Write:
How do you think you are participating in God's plans?

What I am about to say is a difficult but true statement: What we are experiencing is a part of God's plan.

Life happens because we are human, and there are certain things that are beyond our control. We can't control genetics or how the systems in our body fail or become overreactive. Many of us wish we could clear the protein built up in our loved one's brain so they can keep their memory. All of it is now in the hands of God.

Our physical death is a price we must pay for sins of man. However, our spiritual bodies have a home in New Jerusalem. Jesus came and endured the crucifixion to pay for our sins. He rose with authority over all sin and death. He ascended to heaven to prepare a place for us all to dwell forever. We can have that gift of eternal life if we repent and accept Christ as our savior. That's God's divine plan. You and I are included in that divine plan. All of this can be found in the books of the New Testament.

Therefore, what we are enduring now is also a part of the plan he has for our lives. God chose us to be the representation of his loving hands. He chose us to do the best we can for the people we love. He chose us to be the advocates of their care. He chose us to be their champion. He did it because he knew we were the best people for the job. It's not easy, but God made a promise that he would never leave nor forsake us.

We should not worry about failure or feel guilty if we don't get everything right. God said he will listen to our prayers if we trust him and seek him with our whole hearts. He will comfort our hearts and give us everything we need because we are a part of his plans.

So we honor him by giving our dear loved ones and God the best that we have.

Let us pray:

Father, we thank you for having plans for our lives. God, help us to understand our roles in your divine plans for us. Help us to fulfill those roles to the best of our abilities. In your name we pray, Amen.

Day 20

Be Still

"Come and see what the Lord has done, the desolations he has brought on the earth. He makes wars cease to the ends of the earth. He breaks the bow and shatters the spear; he burns the shields with fire. He says, 'Be still, and know that I am God; I will be exalted among the nations, I will be exalted in the earth.' The Lord Almighty is with us; the God of Jacob is our fortress."
—Psalm 46:8-11 (NIV)

Read:
Psalm 46

Write:
How should we be still in our everyday lives? How should we rely on God to fight on our behalf?

I get it. We like to fight our own battles. We love to solve problems on our own. We think we have it all handled.

We don't have it all together, and about some issues we just don't have the answers. However, there is hope and reassurance in knowing we have an amazing God who can do all things and fight those impossible battles for us. We just must be willing to sit still.

Sometimes our own pride and ego can hinder and deter the peace God provides. We waste so much time trying to bend God to do our will instead of yielding to the will and plans God has for us. The sooner we allow God to move on our behalf, the quicker we can abide in God's peace and love. He already has the tools to bring peace to the war in our minds.

Only God can comfort our fears, anxiety, and grief. Only he can place the right people in our lives who can help us cope with the many emotions we deal with daily. Only his love can set us free from the prisons we have placed ourselves in.

He is just waiting for our invitation to do so.

Let us pray:

God, our hero and champion, we thank you for taking up the mantle of fighting our battles for us. We acknowledge that we need you to face the everyday highs and lows. Help us to be still physically and spiritually so we can invite you in to help us overcome our enemies. In your name we pray, Amen.

Day 21

Loving Hands

"So he got up from the table and took off his robes. Picking up a linen towel, he tied it around his waist. Then he poured water into a washbasin and began to wash the disciples' feet, drying them with the towel he was wearing."—John 13:4-5

Read:
John 14:1-19

Write:
How is caring for your loved one like what Jesus did for his disciples?

Providing care means we must do things we never thought we had to do. It's a very humbling job. It's a job that requires a gentle touch and loving hands.

Jesus gave a perfect example of love by washing his disciples' feet. Foot washing in those times was a lowly job and, to be honest, nasty. Think about it. People had only sandals to provide comfort for their feet. So they were exposed to dust and dirt. They also had sweat and oil mixed in. It was a dirty job, but it needed to be done daily so people would not get sick from bacterial and fungal infections.

Jesus did this smelly, stinky job to teach us how to love and serve one another. To inherit the blessings of Abraham and the promises of salvation, we must learn love by doing arduous tasks and work.

My friends, God has given us an opportunity to use our loving hands to minister to our loved ones. Wound care, incontinence care, mobility assistance, helping with meals, and distributing medication are all works of love. Everything we do is a ministry of love. It's challenging work, and sometimes we get stuck in a routine. We must never lose sight of why we are doing this important work.

When we feel stressed or we start to lose sight of that, I suggest we center ourselves in prayer and self-reflection. We cannot lose sight of why we do the things we do for the people we care about.

Let us pray:

Heavenly Father, thank you for allowing your Son to show us many ways to love. Help us to follow his example of love as we continue to care for our loved ones. In your name we pray, Amen.

Day 22

Don't Get Tired of Doing Good

"Let us not get tired of doing good, because in time we'll have a harvest if we don't give up."—Galatians 6:9

Read:
Galatians 6:6-10

Write:
Reflect on how this scripture encourages you.

    In this passage, Paul is reminding us to be encouraged by doing what is right. Doing the work that we do, we often feel like the world is passing us by. Everything is fast-paced, and here we are just sitting in the slow lane. It can be very frustrating because this is not how we planned our life to be.

    To be honest, we are not really missing much. We get something that is priceless and could never be replaced—time. We get time to learn more about our loved ones. We get to watch their favorite shows and movies. We often are happy just to enjoy their presence. All these tiny moments that we take for granted will one day be cherished memories.

    One memory I have is watching a red moon with my dad one spring night before he passed away. We didn't say much. We just looked up at the sky and marveled at what God created. I would redo that in a heartbeat today.

    So we should be glad and not grow weary in the work we do for our loved ones. God is going to reward us with many blessings. Some we may see right away, and others may be delayed.

The time we have with our loved ones is finite. Doing what the Lord called us to do will one day lead to heavenly reward that is infinite.

God sees our work, and so does that world that passes us by. Our stories and work will one day be a source of hope for someone else who will one day do the same thing.

Let us pray:

God, we thank you for keeping your promises. We ask that you continue to guide us as we are doing our labor of love. May we see the fruits of our harvest, and we are praising you in advance for them. In your name we pray, Amen.

Day 23

Time Is Fleeting and Precious

"Teach us to number our days so we can have a wise heart."
—Psalm 90:12

Read:
Psalm 90

Write:
Reflect on how precious time is.

We are so spoiled in life that we always think we have enough time. So we put things off. We always say, "I'll get to it tomorrow" or "I've still got time." We really don't know if we will have tomorrow. Procrastination can get us into trouble and regret if we are not careful.

The psalmist in this chapter has historically been tied to Moses. In this psalm, he reminds us how fleeting and precious time is. We never know when it will be too late. That is why it is important to cherish each day like it is our last day. Whatever it is God has placed on our heart to say or do, we must make the effort to do as soon as possible. That "tomorrow" will turn into a week, a month, a year, or even a decade, and we still will have left God's work undone.

We don't know how much time we have left with our loved ones, especially those whose illness is serious. So we must share and show how much we love our family while we still have breath and ability. One day we will have to say goodbye, and it will be too late. Our hearts will be full of regret and guilt.

We should never squander a day God has blessed us with. We should honor him by living each day to our best potential.

Let us pray:
God, help us to number our days and live them wisely. Help us not postpone our potential and live life to the best of our ability. May the time we spend caring for others foster memories that will last for generations to come. In your name we pray, Amen.

Day 24

Thank You

"Rejoice always. Pray continually. Give thanks in every situation because this is God's will for you in Christ Jesus."—1 Thessalonians 5:16-18

Read:
1 Thessalonians 5:16-18

Write:
Share about what and who you are thankful for on this journey.

"Thank you" are two simple words, but they truly mean a lot. They can really make someone's day. "Thank you" is an acknowledgement that we notice something was done for us. It shows we are appreciative of the work and sacrifice done. One "thank you" can change someone's day.

We give thanks to God for all his bountiful blessings that he give us each day. We show our appreciation through worship, service, music, dance, prayer, giving, and so many other ways, though we know we can never fully repay God for his unwavering love and grace.

We also thank God by honoring and caring for our loved ones. They bring us so much joy, and by dedicating our time and energy to them, it's our way of thanking them and him.

What we do can seem like a thankless job. However, it is not. On behalf of your loved ones, I say, "Thank you." Thank you for the long nights and early mornings. Thank you for the transportation to medical appointments. Thank you for providing the help and resources your loved ones need every day. Your gift of love is appreciated, and God knows and sees the challenging work you do. You are making a difference.

Sometimes it is hard, but you have always managed to get it done. If you don't hear this today, "Thank you so much."

Let us pray:

Father, we come with hearts full of thanksgiving. We owe all of who we are to you. We thank you for choosing us to be caregivers. We thank you for giving us the means and the ability to do so. In your name we pray, Amen.

Day 25

Seek Jesus in All Things

"Ask, and you will receive. Search, and you will find. Knock, and the door will be opened to you. For everyone who asks, receives. Whoever seeks, finds. And to everyone who knocks, the door is opened."—Matthew 7:7-8

Read:
Matthew 7:7-12

Write:
What should you pray or ask God for in this season?

What are you seeking God for in this time frame of your life? Is it peace, strength, wisdom, understanding, grace, love, or all the above?

I get it. It's hard to take on this responsibility. I know firsthand how overwhelming it can be. It can be so much easier to do it if we seek Jesus first. He can provide all we need.

In Matthew 7:7-12, Jesus teaches us that if we go to him and the Father and earnestly ask what is on our heart, they will provide it to us. They will not withhold it from us because we are his children. We are saved by grace, and we have accepted Christ as lord. Therefore, like a child loved by a parent, we too can go to our heavenly parent asking for what we long.

We must learn to seek Jesus first during our tough times, especially when caring for a loved one. Godly council and help will carry us further than what the world can offer. There is nothing that can compare to the vast amount of love, hope, and resources God has for us. He won't deny them to us, and he will always have an answer for us when we pray.

God already knows his plans for us, and he is working things out for us in his own way. We just must fully rely on him.

Let us pray:

Heavenly Father, we thank you for always being a kind, listening ear and a provider. Help us to continue to pursue you and your love. Help us to continue to seek you when life gets tough. In your name we pray, Amen.

Day 26

Stay Connected to the True Vine

"Remain in me, and I will remain in you. A branch can't produce fruit by itself, but must remain in the vine. Likewise, you can't produce fruit unless you remain in me. I am the vine; you are the branches. If you remain in me and I in you, then you will produce much fruit. Without me, you can't do anything."
—John 15:4-5

Read:
John 15:1-8

Write:
Reflect on how you can stay connected with God even as you are caring for your loved one.

It's particularly important to stay connected and rooted in Jesus as we care for our loved ones. We can easily slip up and forget to fit in God the Father, God the Son, and God the Holy Spirit in our tight schedules. If we fail to acknowledge, honor, and worship God daily, we lose our connection to the true vine—Jesus.

Yes, this work can be cumbersome and tiring. We may not be able to go to church and Bible study in person. However, that does not exclude us from being close to Jesus and understanding his perfect plan for our lives. We still have a personal responsibility to take care of our spiritual development. That means we must find some time to do our own personal study and prayer every day.

We cannot accomplish much without the power of God and the guidance of his Son and Spirit. Our branches have the capability to yield much fruit, but is it good fruit? Are they the fruits of the Spirit?

This job we have is a serious one. We are entrusted with the care of other human beings. We are called to be our best, and the only way we can be our best is by following God's best example, Jesus.

Our study, our worship, our witness, and our personal development are key to our ability to give the best care to our loved ones.

Let us pray:

Lord of the harvest, we are thankful to be connected to you. Prune our branches and cultivate us to your will. May the fruits that we bear be a blessing to our family, our church, and our community. Help us to stay connected to you always. In your name, Amen.

Day 27

May the Work of Our Hands Last

"Let the kindness of the Lord our God be over us. Make the work of our hands last. Make the work of our hands last!"—Psalm 90:17

Read:
Psalm 90

Write:
How do you feel about your ministry of caring for your loved one? Is it another job or a labor of love?

Yes, my friends, we are back in Psalm 90. A few days ago, we focused on numbering our days. Today we are focusing on our work as an impression on those we serve.

Being a caretaker can be another full-time job with the scheduling of appointments, the weekly refill of medications, the treatment regimens, the getting them up, the laying them down, and the dealing with the emotional toll it requires.

Moses concludes this prayer with our focal scripture. It was so important that he said it twice. That is an insightful thing to pray for—to make the work of our hands last. This labor of love that we do does have an impression. It could leave our loved ones with the best quality of the lives they have left, or it could add to their suffering.

It's vital we remember why we have been called to do this work. God chose us because we were our loved ones' best options. He knows we have the capacity to make sure their latter days are some of the best days of their lives. Our work is an extension of God's love and our love for them. We set the example we would like our children and other family members to follow.

That's why we must strive to make a great and long-lasting impression. Yes, it can be tough at times. However, the quality of the work we put in will speak for us.

We as believers of Christ should be sure it speaks of love and dedication.

Let us pray:

God, thank you for the ability to be able to work with our hands. May our loving hands be an example of your love and mercy toward us. May our labor of love reflect the examples you showed us through your son, Jesus. In your name we pray, Amen.

Day 28

Trust the Spirit in Tough situations

"In the same way, the Spirit comes to help our weakness. We don't know what we should pray, but the Spirit himself pleads our case with unexpressed groans."
—Romans 8:26

Read:
Romans 8:18-26

Write:
Reflect on what Paul is saying about how we should face difficult seasons.

If anyone knew about tough seasons and hardships, it would be Paul. Snake bites, shipwrecks, beatings, and imprisonment are just a few things he faced while sharing the good news with the world. In Romans 8, he gives us words of encouragement on how we as believers should rely on God's spirit to give us comfort.

In our journey as caregivers, we are often faced with difficult seasons. We are often bombarded with one thing after the next. Sometimes our emotions are all over the place. One moment we are OK, and the next we could be crying our eyes out. At times when we pray, we have so much to say. In other moments, we don't have the words to express the pain we feel.

When we are in that season, the Spirit who lives in us has the words to speak to God on our behalf.

The Holy Spirit is a gift awakened in all believers on the day of Pentecost. Jesus foretold how impactful and powerful it would be in John 14:16-20. He promised this gift would be a comforter and a guide who would keep us and sustain us. He said he lives in us all because we have accepted Jesus to be our savior. This gift is our voice, and it is our inspiration to keep going. It is the fire that fuels the work we do.

When we sit all alone crying, he interprets our tears so Jesus and our Father can understand them. His presence give us hope for tomorrow.

When the next tough day or tough season comes, let us remember to look to the Spirit to be that beacon of hope.

Let us pray:

Heavenly Father, we thank you for the gift of the Holy Spirt. May we continue to rely on him as our voice when we can't speak. Help us to lean on you during our difficult days. In your name we pray, Amen.

Day 29

Be Godly with the Elderly

"Don't correct an older man, but encourage him like he's your father; treat younger men like your brothers, treat older women like your mother, and treat younger women like your sisters with appropriate respect."
—1 Timothy 5:1-2

Read:
1 Timothy 5:1-17

Write:
Reflect on how you are interacting with the elderly in your care or everyday encounters.

The next two days we will be focusing on 1 Timothy 5. Paul offers Timothy very insightful advice: The elders in our lives are precious jewels, and they have so much wisdom and love to give.

A lot of you reading this are like me—a caregiver for a parent. Some may even be blessed to care for a grandparent. It's our duty to do our best for them while God gives us the opportunity to do so.

We often want to treat older people as frail and in the way. That's not entirely true. Some elderly people have more energy and strength than most, and their minds are still sharp. They may not move as fast, and they take their time to get where they are going. However, they are still relevant and important to our families. Their wealth of knowledge and experience is a gift to us that we should cherish.

I do realize most of us are now seeing that vibrance starting to fade and that they may need a little help. We should only offer that help when it is needed and allow them the independence they still have.

For those who are at the stage of life where they are fully reliant on our help, remember to do it with kindness, compassion, empathy, and love. Soon, with God's favor, we will be at that age as well, and we would want the same care and respect.

So while God gives us the opportunity, let us give our seniors the best quality of life we can.

Let us pray:
Father, we thank you for the gift of growing older. Help us to love and care for our elders and keep them safe. Help us to offer them grace and continue to be whatever they need us to be for them. In your name we pray, Amen.

Day 30

Our Service Is a Symbol of Our Love and Faith

"But if someone doesn't provide for their own family, and especially for a member of their household, they have denied the faith. They are worse than those who have no faith."—1 Timothy 5:8

Read:
1 Timothy 5:1-17 (again)

Write:
How do you feel your act of love is also a symbol of your faith to God?

Faith is not just what we do on the day we celebrate our sabbath. It's also what we do every single day.

Our faith is a symbol of our love for God. We can't say we love God and not show that same love and respect to the people he blessed us with. A lack of love and respect is the opposite of the faith we profess. God is love. That means we must show that same godly love to each other.

Sadly, there are family dynamics all over the world where there is a lack of love and empathy. People grow up in broken homes, or they have experienced trauma that can cause people not to respect their family. They also could become people who never truly experience agape (godly) love in their lives. That can lead to more abuse and neglect, and the cycle continues.

The love of Jesus is the only thing that can break that cycle.

Jesus was and still is the perfect example of faith and love. We as caregivers should emulate and reciprocate that love to our loved ones. They need to witness and experience it. It is essential to their healing and recovery. It is also essential to our faith walk. By showing our love to others, our faith in God is put into action. By doing this, people around us can see Christ in us.

I know the work that we do is difficult, but our story will one day be someone's testimony. Our love is one of the greatest ways to express our faith to others.

Let us pray:

Heavenly Father, thank you for showing us what faith really is by sending us your son to be the ultimate example. We pray we don't deny our faith in you by withholding our love and responsibility to our loved ones. Give us the strength to do the work we are called to do. In your name we pray, Amen.

Day 31

A Plan for Saying Farewell

"There's a season for everything and a time for every matter under the heavens: a time for giving birth and a time for dying, a time for planting and a time for uprooting what was planted."—Ecclesiastes 3:1-2

Read:
Ecclesiastes 3:1-8

Write:
Reflect on how you feel about saying goodbye to a loved one. Have you talked to your loved one about their wishes?

One thing that is certain is having to say goodbye to people we love. Death is a subject we don't want to discuss. We dread it. We want to keep the conversations away from our minds as long as possible.

However, as responsible caregivers, we must take the time to plan for the time to say goodbye.

I didn't really have that conversation with my dad. His illness took an unexpected turn for the worse, and the plans he had for his end of life were left undone because he thought he had more time.

We did our best to give him a celebration of life that expressed our love for him. We had a road map from previous experiences of dealing with death, so it was a little easier.

So I encourage you all to have meaningful conversations with your loved ones while you still have time. That way you don't have to make such tough decisions while grieving.

I have a few suggestions: Get a notebook and jot down important things and contact numbers. Find out what their favorite songs and hymns are. What is their favorite color? What did they enjoy doing in life? How do they want their live celebrated? It's also important to consider estate planning and how they want their assets allocated. These small steps can be immensely helpful to your loved ones.

Since death is an important aspect of caregiving, the next few days of our time together will focus on how to deal with grief and saying goodbye. These are based off my individual experiences, and I understand that death can be difficult and different from my experiences. These are some things I wish I knew as I helped care for my father.

The most important thing to remember in all of this is that God is and will continue to be with us during this time whenever it comes. Our faith in and relationship with him will sustain us and keep us.

Let us pray:

Father, we thank you for all the seasons in our lives. We thank you for being our source of peace and comfort when we are in those difficult seasons. Guide us with love and grace as we prepare for what is to come. In your name we pray, Amen.

Day 32

Now What?

"A time for crying and a time for laughing, a time for mourning and a time for dancing, a time for throwing stones and a time for gathering stones, a time for embracing and a time for avoiding embraces."
—*Ecclesiastes 3:4-5*

Read:
Ecclesiastes 3:1-8 (again)

Write:
How would you like to spend your last days with your loved one? What can you do to make it special?

There may come a time that a medical professional will come and say, "We have done all that we can do. All we can do is make them comfortable," or, "They only have so many weeks or months to live."

Those are words no one wants to hear. You are left feeling sad, confused, and a little hopeless. You may even ask yourself, "Now what?"

In those moments, we must find some way to just pray and seek the guidance of God. I know some people don't want to talk to or hear from God at that moment because as humans, we want to place the blame on him. Some of us may ask "Why?"

The only way we can get all those questions answered is through prayer and meditation.

Like I stated a few days ago, time is precious and fleeting. So what time we do have should be used to create as many memories as possible.

When I was told about my father, I spent those last hours talking to him. I wasn't sure if he heard me, but it gave me a since of peace knowing I took the time to do so. In those conversations, a ministry was birthed, and it has touched the lives of many because of it. Those last moments pushed me to spend these forty days with you.

It is also helpful to get your emotions out. If you need to cry, then cry. If you need to write in a journal, then write until you can't anymore. If you need to yell at the top of your lungs, go for it. This grief journey is yours.

It's not healthy for anyone to hold in their emotions and not deal with them. The stress and toll it will cause on our body will not be helpful.

By relieving that tension and stress, it will open our minds and souls to voice of God. That voice will give us the directions we need to navigate what to do next.

Let us pray:

Father, we thank you for being that still and calming voice in the middle of our personal storms. Help us to navigate through the choppy waters and focus on the next phase of the journey. When we feel weak, lift us up. When we feel alone, comfort us. Be the lighthouse that guides us to shore. In your name we pray, Amen.

Day 33

This Is Not Our Home

"We know that if the tent that we live in on earth is torn down, we have a building from God. It's a house that isn't handmade, which is eternal and located in heaven. We groan while we live in this residence. We really want to dress ourselves with our building from heaven."—2 Corinthians 5:1-2

Read:
2 Corinthians 5:1-10

Write:
How do you feel about eternal life and earthly death after reading this passage?

In this passage and many other passages of scripture, Paul writes about death bringing the final reward and victory for those who claim Christ as their Lord and Savior. In some cases, Paul longed to be with Jesus in heaven.

In this passage, Paul compares our earthly bodies to tents. Tents are not permanent structures. They are frail and can get worn down. Eventually the cloth will fade, and its integrity will deteriorate, meaning that whoever dwells in a tent will have to find a new place to dwell.

That analogy fits our lives so well. We, too, will soon have to deal with a frail body that slowly deteriorates, and one day our souls will no longer be able to be free in our earthly bodies. Paul states that if we claim our salvation through Jesus, we will inherit a new body in heaven. We will be free to serve God and not worry about the needs of our old bodies. We will no longer be in pain or sickness. We will be so focused on praising God that nothing else will matter.

As we care for our dear loved ones whose bodies are failing or have failed, we can find joy in knowing this is not their final destination. Jesus in John 14 said he was going to prepare a place for us. Those are the hands that will build our new bodies, and they will not wear out. We will be sad if we have to say goodbye, but we can rejoice in knowing our loved ones are no longer suffering from the pains of this world. We can be at peace knowing they are free from the weight they carried down here.

Earth and this body are our temporary residence. It is imperative that we work on building a relationship with Jesus so we can one day have our permanent residence with him.

As we work hard to make sure our loved ones are comfortable, we are also preparing our souls for when we must take that journey as well.

Let us pray:

Heavenly Father, we thank you for preparing a permanent dwelling place for us. As we prepare our souls to be ready for it, help us to fulfill the work we must do on this side of heaven. We thank you for sending us Jesus as our advocate, teacher, and friend to show us the way home. We thank you for your Holy Spirit to be our guide and source of comfort on our journey back to permanent residence with you. In your name we pray, Amen.

Day 34

Your Heart Will Heal

"The Lord is close to the brokenhearted; he saves those whose spirits are crushed."—Psalm 34:18

Read:
Psalm 34:15-18

Write:
Reflect on your emotions about losing or potentially losing a loved one.

Mourning someone you love and care for deeply is hard. It's like having a wound in your heart that just won't heal. One moment you are happy, and then the next you feel like crying.

It is especially tough on caregivers. When you have been doing a labor of love for so long and suddenly that ministry stops, it can make you feel lost and sad. For some, it can lead to self-guilt and depression.

These emotions are a part of life, and thankfully we have a loving God who can mend broken hearts.

The psalmist states that God is close to those who have broken hearts. How can we know he is close? We remember who he is and what tools he has provided for us. He has given us the gift of the Holy Spirit to be our comforter and guide. He gave us his son, Jesus, to be a friend and advocate in our times for sorrow. He provided us with his holy word that has been crafted and handed down from generation to generation to show us the promises he made to us.

Pain of loss that we may one day feel or still feel is unavoidable. We can be assured because God has never turned away from his promises to us. When we forget those promises, we should seek guidance in reading scripture and by praying. When we still need clarity about how we are feeling, it is OK to seek spiritual or professional guidance. God has gifted people who can help us navigate how to deal with our grief.

God will still love us if we need to talk to someone about our emotions. He wants us whole again. He wants us to continue the excellent work he has called us to do.

Let us pray:
Heavenly Father, we thank you for standing by us during the challenging times in our lives. We thank you that we have the power of your word, the comfort of your loving arms, the friendship of Jesus, and the guidance of your spirit. We know that with these provisions, we can find healing for our broken hearts. In your name we pray, Amen.

Day 35

Get Plenty of Rest

"When Jesus heard about John, he withdrew in a boat to a deserted place by himself."—Matthew 14:13

Read:
Matthew 14:1-13

Write:
How can you follow Jesus's example of resting in grief?

When the time comes to say goodbye, things can be busy and stressful. Being the primary caregiver usually means the lot falls on you to help with the final arrangements. When all is said and done and the last amen is finished, grief sets in. The phone calls cease, and the visits from family become fewer.

From the experiences I had, you will hit a wall of emotions that can be daunting to deal with. When it comes, it's a sign you need to steal away and be with God.

In my case, I couldn't immediately take a break because my mom was in the hospital and my cousin had a stroke on the day of my father's funeral. I had to deal with getting Mom out of the hospital and comforting my cousin who couldn't be in New York with her brother.

Instead of taking a monthlong break from work, I only took a couple of weeks. I didn't listen to my body; I wanted to stay busy to quiet my mind.

I'm telling you today: When your time comes, take as long as needed to rest.

When Jesus heard about the death of his dear cousin and friend, John the Baptist, Jesus took a break to grieve. He was divine, but he still had a well of emotions for John, and he took the responsibility to deal with them by being in solitude.

That quiet time is a needed break that our mind, body, and soul need to begin the healing process. Grief takes a toll on us. For us to be effective and available, we must listen to our bodies.

The last thing anyone needs is to have a health scare that can hinder the next chapter of life God has for us. We are human, not robots. God will restore and recharge us.

Let us pray:

Heavenly Father, thank you for being an example of resting during our grief. Help us to find peace in our hearts so we can continue to be effective in the ministry we are called to do. Help us to be still and know who you are. In your name we pray, Amen.

Day 36

Restoration Is Coming

"After you have suffered for a little while, the God of all grace, the one who called you into his eternal glory in Christ Jesus, will himself restore, empower, strengthen, and establish you."
—1 Peter 5:10

Read:
1 Peter 5:6-11

Write:
Reflect on what restoration means to you.

Restoration is a word no one really thinks about when it comes to grieving. I say this because when we lose a loved one, we feel like we lose a part of ourselves. It feels like a huge void in our lives or a wound that does not heal. We will never be the same.

If you think about a restoration project of any kind, nothing is the same. It becomes enhanced and better than the original version of that object or area.

Even amid grief, God can empower us, strengthen us, and uplift us. God can take our broken hearts and mend them. He can give us the resolve to keep pushing toward wholeness. We can't do it by ourselves. God, the expert builder, will have to have his hands on the project the entire time.

Jesus, the primary carpenter, knows the floor plan. He will throw out sadness and replace it with joy. He will put in support beams where we are weak. He will carefully nurse the wounds this loss has or will have on our lives. He will keep his promise that he will never leave us.

The Holy Spirt will put in the final additions by lighting up the spaces in our heart. He does so by mounting God's word on our hearts. This makes our heart warm and inviting and more comfortable.

By doing these things, God is placing us on a path to being restored.

Let us pray:

Heavenly Father, we thank you for your power to make us new. We thank you for being the expert builder of our lives. Keep us in the hollow of your hand and shape us into the gifted and anointed individuals you have called us to be. In your name we pray, Amen.

Day 37

Grief Will Not Be Your Identity

"I'm convinced that nothing can separate us from God's love in Christ Jesus our Lord: not death or life, not angels or rulers, not present things or future things, not powers or height or depth, or any other thing that is created."
—*Romans 8:38-39*

Read:
Romans 8:31-39

Write:
How do you feel about who you are now in Christ? Do you think it's good or bad?

My friends, this is another reminder that death is not the end. The pain we feel or soon will feel from losing our loved ones will be replaced with joy. This feeling of sorrow is not who we are or will be. We are children of the promise God made to Abraham. We are redeemed by the promise keeper, Jesus Christ. We are made a new creation in God's divine image. The passing of loved ones is not the end but only the next phase of the promise.

We can very easily slip into a deep depression, or we can become angry and vengeful with God, over the death of our loved ones. We may even feel like God has abandoned us.

However, that is far from the truth. Nothing can separate us from God and his love for us. God did not do this as a punishment or out of spite. He knew our loved ones were tired and needed rest. He did not take them away from us, but he gave our loved ones a refuge and much-needed relief from suffering.

He also saw the toll the work we were doing took on our minds, bodies, and souls.

It's important to seek comfort and advice from God and like-minded people of faith during this season of our lives. Their guidance and wise counsel will help us see our futures are filled with so much hope and promise. We don't want to lose ourselves in our emotions. We should not close ourselves off from the world and lose focus on what is next for us.

God still has a calling on our lives. We still have a family to provide for. We still have dreams and goals to accomplish. There is still more to do in the land of the living.

One day in the New Jerusalem, we will be reunited with all the saints of God and the Holy Triune God. Until that day comes, we are called to heal so we can help others heal in the future.

Let us pray:

Dear promise keeper God, we thank you for providing us love and grace as we work in this labor of love. When the time comes to say goodbye, help us to not turn inward to ourselves. Help us to seek your face and to find help from our neighbors to heal and evolve. Guide us with your Holy Spirit to navigate the terrains of grief. May our journey become our testimony for others who follow. In your name we pray, Amen.

Day 38

Find a New Ministry to Do

*"Don't remember the prior things; don't ponder ancient history. Look!
I'm doing a new thing; now it sprouts up; don't you recognize it?
I'm making a way in the desert, paths in the wilderness."*
—*Isaiah 43:18-19*

Read:
Isaiah 43:18-19

Write:
What do you want to do besides being a caregiver? What are some passions tugging at your heart?

Dealing with someone who has passed away or is in transition can be and will be tough. It has been two years for me, and I still have my bad days.

The most important thing to remember is that God is and will always be good to you and your family. You will not always tear up or be emotional. You will come out of this journey better than you went in. God wants us to purge our sadness and focus that energy into something new and special. He told an exiled Israel to forget the feelings and emotions of the past and focus on something new.

So I ask you today: What will be your next phase after being a caretaker for so long? What is God showing you that he wants you to do? For those who are caring for more than one family member, what can you do differently that will revitalize you to want to keep going?

God does not want us to dwell on the past. He wants us to trust him with our future. He still has a purpose and a calling on our lives. He wants to do something fresh with us.

Now my friends, that does not mean we suppress our grief or not allow ourselves grace for when we do have unresolved feelings and emotions. It is important to feel and to work through what we are feeling. But we should not let those emotions be our prison. God wants us to be free, and Jesus came so that we can be free. The Holy Spirit is present with us now to help us stay free and to help us navigate our lives toward a better future.

As I was drafting this book, a new opportunity arose for my life in service to God. It looks like a situation where I feel like I can grow and make a difference.

I'm thankful I kept my heart open to new opportunities to serve. All the mistakes, pitfalls, heartaches, and setbacks I experienced while taking care of my father and now my mother did not break me. They showed me God is still good. It refined my faith and established the foundation for the new thing I am doing.

God wants to do the same for you, too.

Let us pray:

Heavenly Father, thank you for wanting to do a new thing within us. Help us to keep our hearts open in our grief and our continuing to care for our loved ones. Thank you for setting us free from the exile of our emotions. Help us to listen to you when you call us to do that new thing. May the work that we do in that new season be a blessing to those who are seeking it. In your name we pray, Amen.

Day 39

Remember the Professionals Who Helped You

"We always thank God for all of you when we mention you constantly in our prayers."—1 Thessalonians 1:2

Read:
1 Thessalonians 1:2-10

Write:
Reflect on who you want to express gratitude to who helped you and your family through these challenging times.

I always say you must have a kind and loving heart to be a health-care worker. These people must have the resolve and stamina to witness so much. Many become more like family instead of just someone who is doing their job. Their warm smile and bedside demeanor is something to cherish. They often pour so much out, and they rarely put anything back in their cups.

That is why it is imperative that we tell and show these people how much they mean to our families. Their care and love helped.

So I suggest you do something special for the special people who helped along the way. A card, a gift, or a meal can really go a long way. The doctors, nurses, home health aides, and CNAs are gifts from God. When we show our gratitude to them, we pour back into their cups of blessings. They chose this profession because they want to help people, and it brings them joy to know that they did. So often they hurt just as much as we do when a loved one passes because of the bonds that are developed.

Our prayers are just as important to them as well. Even if they share different beliefs or have not been in church for a while, we can still do our part to pray for them. It doesn't have to be a public or long prayer. If it is genuine and sincere, I think it will help them in some form or fashion.

Our kindness and thankfulness will be important in this stage of care, because often we must lean on each other.

Let us pray:
God, we thank you for the gifts of the health-care team you blessed us with. We thank you for their training and dedication to their profession. We thank you for their smile and loving hands. We ask that you cover them with love and care as they continue in your work. In your name we pray, Amen.

Day 40

Find the Good in This Season

"We know that God works all things together for good for the ones who love God, for those who are called according to his purpose."—Romans 8:28

Read:
Romans 8:26-30

Write:
How can you use your story to help others who may be experiencing the same things you have?

Believe it or not, God can use us to do amazing things in tough situations. He wants to do the same thing for us and through us. He wants us to see what he sees in this situation that we are in. He wants us to see that despite all we have endured, he is still good, he is still present, and he is still God. He wants us to look past the hurt and all the mess that comes with being a caregiver and see what we can build with it.

This journey of love and faith that we are on together came out of my grief. Those of you who are fans of my work know that my second book of poems were about the health journey I took with my father and how I dealt with his unexpected passing from cancer. I took what I was feeling and typed it out on my cell phone in between doctor's appointments. While I waited for him, I wrote.

When I saw that my dad's healing would come through his passing, I made a promise to him that I would finish what I started. Through many tearful sessions of writing, I got it done. It's not on the *New York Times* bestseller's list yet, but so many people have told me they needed to read the words I wrote.

So my friends, this journey that we are on will lead to something better. It will lead to something great. One day the mourning will turn to dancing (Psalm 30:11). The tears we sow will be the water for new seeds of ministry in our lives. Our healing will someday lead to someone else to their healing. I have a feeling that in whatever form your ministry manifests itself, it will bless so many others.

It has been a great forty days to grow together in faith and love. I hope God will bless you and your loved ones. I pray he will continue to bless you and keep you wherever your journey may lead.

I also pray your test will soon be a testimony.

Let us pray:

Most gracious and loving God, we thank you for this journey of faith together. We thank you for the inspiration and the guidance of your Holy Spirit. May his presence continue to help and comfort us in the days to come. In your name we pray, Amen.

About the Author

Stephon Carlisle Void, a native of Bowman, South Carolina, is a dedicated and accomplished professional with a passion for community service, faith, and writing.

Stephon is an honors graduate of Bowman High School and holds a Bachelor of Science in biology, as well as a Master of Science in biotechnology, both from Claflin University in Orangeburg, South Carolina. He has spent fifteen years at Claflin University, where he currently serves as a nuclear magnetic resonance technician in the Department of Chemistry.

In addition to his professional endeavors, Stephon is an active member of New Covenant United Methodist Church in Bowman, South Carolina, where he has held the role of Certified Lay Servant for twenty years. His dedication to the church and his community is unwavering, and he finds fulfillment in various roles, including singing in the choir, engaging in community outreach, teaching Sunday school, and leading children and youth moments on Sundays. He also serves on the Orangeburg District Committee of the Superintendency and the Orangeburg District Lay Servant Ministries. He is currently the district lay leader for the Orangeburg District of the South Carolina Conference of The United Methodist Church.

Stephon's love for writing blossomed when he was selected as a contributing author for the "Africana II" worship series produced by Discipleship Ministries of The United Methodist Church. His work was featured throughout the 2020-2021 calendar year. He has also published his first book, *From My Heart to Your Eyes: Poems of Faith and Social Justice*, available for purchase through the Advocate Press. His second book, *A Healing Journey: Poems of Faith, Healing, Grief, and Recovery*, was published in April 2023 by the Advocate Press and received recognition in *The Times and Democrat*, the *Get Your Spirit in Shape* podcast, and from the WLTX News 19 Street Squad.

In his leisure time, Stephon enjoys the company of family and friends, cherishing the moments he spends with them. He currently resides in Bowman, with his mother, Shirlene Void, and continues to be a positive force in both his local community and the broader church community.

www.ingramcontent.com/pod-product-compliance
Lightning Source LLC
Chambersburg PA
CBHW022118090426
42743CB00008B/908